2007

DATE DUE

DEMCO INC. 38-2931

The History of Depression

The Mind–Body Connection

ANTIDEPRESSANTS

ANTIDEPRESSANTS

The History of Depression

The Mind–Body Connection

by Kenneth McIntosh

Mason Crest Publishers

Philadelphia

Mason Crest Publishers Inc.
370 Reed Road
Broomall, Pennsylvania 19008
(866) MCP-BOOK (toll free)

First printing
1 2 3 4 5 6 7 8 9 10
Library of Congress Cataloging-in-Publication Data

McIntosh, Kenneth, 1959-
   The history of depression : the mind-body connection / by Kenneth McIntosh.
      p. cm.— (Antidepressants)
   Includes bibliographical references and index.
   ISBN 1-4222-0104-X   ISBN (series) 1-4222-0094-9
   1.   Depression, Mental—History—Juvenile literature. 2.   Antidepressants—History—Juvenile literature. I. Title. II. Series.
   RC537.M3945 2007
   616.85'27061—dc22
                            2006015613

Interior design by MK Bassett-Harvey.
Interiors produced by Harding House Publishing Service, Inc.
www.hardinghousepages.com.
Cover design by Peter Culatta.
Printed in the Hashemite Kingdom of Jordan.

Contents

Introduction

by Andrew M. Kleiman, M.D.

From ancient Greece through the twenty-first century, the experience of sadness and depression is one of the many that define humanity. As long as human beings have felt emotions, they have endured depression. Experienced by people from every race, socioeconomic class, age group, and culture, depression is an emotional and physical experience that millions of people suffer each day. Despite being described in literature and music; examined by countless scientists, philosophers, and thinkers; and studied and treated for centuries, depression continues to remain as complex and mysterious as ever.

In today's Western culture, hearing about depression and treatments for depression is common. Adolescents in particular are bombarded with information, warnings, recommendations, and suggestions. It is critical that adolescents and young people have an understanding of depression and its impact on an individual's psychological and physical health, as well as the treatment options available to help those who suffer from depression.

Why? Because depression can lead to poor school performance, isolation from family and friends, alcohol and drug abuse, and even suicide. This doesn't have to be the case, since many useful and promising treatments exist to relieve the suffering of those with depression. Treatments for depression may also pose certain risks, however.

Since the beginning of civilization, people have been trying to alleviate the suffering of those with depression. Modern-day medicine and psychology have taken the understanding and treatment of depression to new heights. Despite their shortcomings, these treatments have helped millions and millions of people lead happier, more fulfilling and prosperous lives that would not be possible in generations past. These treatments, however, have their own risks, and for some people, may not be effective at all. Much work in neuroscience, medicine, and psychology needs to be done in the years to come.

Many adolescents experience depression, and this book series will help young people to recognize depression both in themselves and in those around them. It will give them the basic understanding of the history of depression and the various treatments that have been used to combat depression over the years. The books will also provide a basic scientific understanding of depression, and the many biological, psychological, and alternative treatments available to someone suffering from depression today.

Each person's brain and biology, life experiences, thoughts, and day-to-day situations are unique. Similarly, each individual experiences depression and sadness in a unique way. Each adolescent suffering from depression thus requires a distinct, individual treatment plan that best suits his or her needs. This series promises to be a vital resource for helping young people recognize and understand depression, and make informed and thoughtful decisions regarding treatment.

Chapter 1

Depression Defined

*T*here's no crispness to the morning. The smell of coffee serves only as a reminder that another long, dreary day has begun. There's no real feeling, no joy, not even much anger, only emptiness. It's difficult to remember feeling any different and getting more difficult to go on feeling this way. . . . A leaden haze obscures the day and folds into a dark tunnel with no hint of light at the end. Where is hope? There is none. Where is happiness? Gone as if it had never been, replaced by tears that must be hidden.

—a physician describes his feelings of depression,
    quoted in *Understanding Depression* by
    Patricia Ainsworth, M.D.

Depression: Hopeless Feelings and a Weary Body

Audrey feels hopelessly unhappy. She has trouble sleeping, and in the morning, she drags herself out of bed. Even little everyday things—brushing her teeth, getting dressed, getting to school—seem difficult. She used to hang out with friends after school, but now she feels so exhausted she comes straight home and goes to bed. She doesn't understand why she feels so down all the time, and when kids at school say, "Snap out of it!" she gets angry. At first, her mom thinks this is just "a teenage thing," but then she realizes Audrey isn't just in a bad mood; she is struggling with something deeper and longer lasting than a case of "the blues." Audrey's mom thinks they had better see a counselor.

Maybe you can relate to some of the above. You may be reading this book because you or a friend suffers from depression. If so, hopefully, this book will provide some helpful insights. If you struggle with depression, you are not alone. On any given day, approximately 121 million people worldwide suffer from depression, and every year in the United States, approximately one in ten people will struggle with the disease. Annually, the costs of depressive illnesses take between thirty-three and forty-four billion dollars out of the U.S. economy.

The Road Ahead

The good news is that most cases of depression—even major depression—can be effectively treated. So even if your feel-

Depressed Celebrities

Even brilliant and successful people struggle with depression. For example:

Abraham Lincoln, president
Audrey Hepburn, actress
Brian Wilson, composer (Beach Boys)
Dick Clark, entertainer (American Bandstand)
Eric Clapton, blues-rock musician
Ellen DeGeneres, comedian, actress
Joan of Arc, French leader
Kurt Cobain, rock star
Ludwig von Beethoven, composer
Mark Twain, author
Mother Teresa of Calcutta, religious worker and humanitarian
Napoleon Bonaparte, emperor
Winona Ryder, actress

ings tell you "this will never get better," the odds are good that your life will improve. Over the past decade, scientists and psychologists have learned a great deal about depression and how to treat it. However, treatment takes time and effort; enlisting the help of mental health professionals might be necessary in the treatment of your depression. You will need to realize there is no "miracle cure" that works equally well for everyone. There are different forms of depression, and each case involves a unique set of factors; what works for your friend or the cure you read about in an article may not help you. Treating the disease takes time, and sometimes it involves trial and error—even with the help of professionals.

More Than Just "the Blues"

"Life is difficult." Those are the first words of *The Road Less Traveled*, by M. Scott Peck, M.D., a best-selling self-help book. As Dr. Peck suggests, we manage life better if we expect to have problems and hurts at times. No one is happy all the time; that's just the way things are. The word "depressed" is often used as a way of saying, "I feel bad." When misfortune strikes—your boyfriend dumps you, you get in an accident, or fail a class—it is normal to feel bad. Even people who never experience **clinical depression** have days when they feel lousy. Sadness is normal.

In this book, the word "depression" means more than just "feeling bad." Occasional sad feelings only last for a short time, and even when feeling a little down in the dumps, people can enjoy sports and social events. In contrast to occasional bad feelings, depression is a mood disorder that influences both mind and body, causing a person to feel profound sadness and a decreased ability to experience pleasure. Furthermore, de-pression influences the entire body, altering patterns of sleep, eating, concentration, exercise, or sex.

Who Gets Depressed?

It might be better to ask, "Who *doesn't* get depressed?" De-pression is no respecter of persons: people of every age, sex,

It's normal to feel sad after an argument with a
boyfriend or girlfriend; depression is a far longer-
lasting and more serious condition.

race, religion, profession, and sexual orientation can suffer from this illness. However, some groups of people are more likely to suffer from depression than others.

Children

Mark was an eleven-year-old who had always done well in school. So his parents were surprised when his teacher requested a parent-teacher conference. At their meeting with the teacher, Mark's parents learned he had been skipping class, picking fights, failing assignments, and doing poorly in his studies. When the teacher tried to talk with Mark about these changes in his behavior, he broke into tears and ran away.

According to experts, children with depression often go unrecognized as adults tend to overlook their symptoms of depressive illness. As in Mark's case, parents or teachers may label these symptoms as "bad behavior." At least 2.5 percent of all children in the United States suffer from depression. Most preteen children will recover within two years, but three-quarters of them will have another episode within five years—and depressive episodes tend to become more severe as children get older.

Teens

Joe, age seventeen, was intelligent and creative, yet he constantly struggled with dark moods. These moods frightened Joe. In an effort to cope with these strange feelings, he began drinking and using illegal drugs. Joe's parents took him for evaluation at an adolescent hospital, where he was diagnosed as having a depressive disorder. A combination of therapy

Suicide: A Teen Epidemic

Each year in the United States, approximately five thousand young people between the ages of fifteen and twenty-four commit suicide. This number has nearly tripled since 1960. Depression and the use of drugs or alcohol may worsen feelings of despair. Teen suicide attempts commonly follow a crisis: loss of a boyfriend or girlfriend, parents' divorce, physical or sexual abuse, or the death of a friend. Danger signs for teen suicide include:

• talking about death and wanting to die

• suicidal thoughts, plans, or fantasies

• previous suicide attempts

• friends who have attempted suicide

• giving away personal possessions

• telling a friend about suicidal plans

• writing a good-bye note

• preoccupation with death

• lack of plans for the future

If you see these signs in a friend, take them seriously and alert an adult. Never leave a suicidal person alone.

The National Suicide Hotline is toll-free and staffed twenty-four hours a day and seven days every week: 1-800-SUICIDE (1-800-784-2433).

and medication stabilized his moods, and he was soon able to enjoy success in school and social life.

A fact sheet from the National Mental Health Association states, "Adolescent depression is increasing at an alarming rate. Recent surveys indicate that as many as one in five teens suffers from clinical depression." Teens (and younger children as well) may experience or express depression as irritability or excessive agitation.

Women

Brooke Shields is an actress and former model. Not long after giving birth to her first child, Shields felt overwhelmed by painful emotions. "I really didn't want to live anymore," she admits. According to the American College of Obstetricians and Gynecologists, **postpartum** depression, the overwhelming sadness that can follow childbirth, may affect as many as one in ten new mothers within six months of delivery. Despite her suffering, Shields was fortunate: medication made a significant difference for the actress, and she was able to return to normal feelings.

Adult women suffer from depression twice as often as men do, and this two-to-one ratio is consistent for women regardless of race, ethnicity, and economic or social status. Experts suggest several reasons why women have more depression. Some think men are simply less likely than women to report depression. Others suggest **sexism** causes women to suffer more. Still others believe women's **hormones** make them more prone to depression: women have more estrogen than men, and they also have more frequent hormonal fluctuations, due to the menstrual cycle, childbirth, birth-control pills, and menopause.

According to the National Mental Health
Association, 20 percent of all teens are depressed.

The Elderly

Marguerite, a ninety-year-old retirement home resident, wonders why she continues living. She says, "All my friends have died, my daughter has died. I can't work, I can't garden . . . what good am I?"

Elderly people are more likely to suffer from depression than are the general public. However, depression is *not* an unavoidable consequence of aging. Some experts believe depression among the elderly increases due to factors such as loneliness, loss of meaningful activities, and lack of adequate exercise. Depression among elderly people who live outside of nursing homes is relatively low (1.8 percent to 2.9 percent), contrasted with 6 percent for those in

The elderly are often more susceptible to depression for a variety of reasons.

nursing home facilities. Older people also tend to be more susceptible than younger people to depression caused by side effects of
medications.

Forms of Mood Disorder

Depression is actually involved in a number of different disorders,
as defined by *The Diagnostic and Statistical Manual of Mental
Disorders, Fourth Edition* (DSM-IV) used by mental health work-
ers. These can be categorized as follows:

- major depressive disorder

- dysthymic disorder (chronic depression)

- bipolar disorder (formerly known as manic-depressive;
  cyclothymic disorder is a less severe form)

- seasonal affective disorder (SAD)

- depression related to hormones (including both premenstrual syndrome and postpartum depression)

Two categories of mood disorders not covered in this book
are mood disorders due to general illness and those caused
by taking drugs. In these cases, depression is a by-product of
other circumstances in the patient's life. Adjustment disorder with depressed mood (reactive depression), caused by unfortunate circumstances in a person's life, is also sometimes
listed as a form of depression.

Major Depressive Disorder

Major depressive disorders involve a very low mood and lack
of interest in pleasures. The change must last for two weeks

or more. Major depression involves a number of the following symptoms, occurring daily:

- inability to concentrate or make decisions
- repeated suicidal thoughts or thoughts of death
- significant changes in sleep patterns, including insomnia
- extreme tiredness, feeling slowed down
- self-loathing, guilt, or feelings of worthlessness
- dramatic changes in eating (either increased or decreased)
- excessive irritability
- sudden and excessive fearfulness

Doctors Charles Elliot and Laura Smith in *Depression for Dummies* describe the awful feelings caused by this illness: "A severe, major episode of depression grabs hold of a person's life and insidiously squeezes out all pleasure . . . severe depression shoves its victims into a dark hole of utter, unrelenting despair."

If your high school has a thousand students, then according to one study (Dr. Peter Lewinsohn, University of Portland, 1996), seventy-seven of them are likely to suffer from major depression in a year. Girls are twice as likely to experience major depression than boys. If you are experiencing several of the symptoms above, you should seek professional help. You may feel like there is no hope—but such feelings are contrary to the facts. Most people with major depression improve with treatment.

Dysthymic Disorder

Dysthymic disorder is usually less severe than major depressive disorder; however, it tends to be longer lasting (chronic). Symptoms may last two years or longer, with the depressed

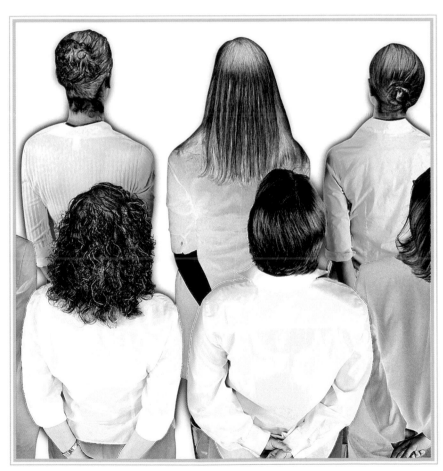

If your high school has a thousand students,
seventy-seven of them are likely to be depressed.

mood occurring most days; the person feels sad more often than she doesn't. Symptoms include:

- trouble concentrating
- low sense of personal worth
- feelings of guilt
- suicidal thoughts
- trouble making decisions
- lack of pleasure in activities
- feelings of hopelessness and sadness
- lethargy

Charlene, for example, couldn't remember feeling joy; she wasn't even sure what "joy" meant. She studied hard and got good grades in school, trying to gain approval and attention, but it seemed her parents didn't even notice her achievements. As an adult, she works hard and earns a big salary, but she still doesn't feel happy. She doesn't realize she suffers from dysthymic depression; she assumes that life is generally unhappy.

People with dysthymic disorder sometimes think "that's just the way life is," so they fail to seek treatment. A majority of people who suffer from untreated dysthymic depression later develop major depression, so it is important to seek treatment. When a person with dysthymia becomes significantly more depressed for a period of time, so that he has crossed the line into a major depressive disorder, this is described as a "double depression."

A person with dysthymic disorder may not
realize she is depressed; instead, she may
assume that life is simply normally joyless.

Bipolar Disorder (Manic-Depressive)

Bipolar disorder is characterized by changes in mood: from excited and energetic to depressed and desolate. A person with this disorder experiences periods of mania, periods with normal, even emotions, and periods of depression. Mania is defined as a week or more in which a person feels "high." She may experience excessive energy, rapid thoughts, an inclination toward taking risks, little need for sleep, and feelings of

A person with bipolar disorder rides an emotional seesaw: first up, then down.

grandiosity; she may start ambitious projects (that she probably won't complete) or even experience delusions.

A less severe form of the same condition is cyclothymic disorder. A person with this disorder also experiences mood swings—but never quite reaches the thresholds of either true mania or depression. Instead, he experiences low-level versions of both: bouts of hypomania (low-level mania) and dysthymia over at least a two-year period.

Amber, fifteen, describes her experiences with bipolar disorder in the book *When Nothing Matters Anymore* by Bev Cobain:

> I've always had angry outbursts. . . . As I got older, my anger worsened. . . . By the time I was thirteen, I was into alcohol and drugs. . . . I knew I was doing bad things, but I never considered the consequences. . . . I saw a doctor who realized I have bipolar disorder, and I was put on **lithium**. I didn't change overnight, but gradually I started feeling different. . . . My brain isn't chaotic anymore. I can sit and have a calm conversation, and I'm in control of my thoughts.

People with bipolar disorder alternate between feeling great, feeling awful, and feeling life is out of control. Manic episodes can involve poor decisions, possibly ruining one's life. People with this disorder also experience higher rates of substance abuse and alcoholism.

Fortunately, most cases can be treated with medication. Some patients, however, enjoy the feeling of mania, so they discontinue medication; they then suffer a relapse of the yo-yo effect of their emotions. The risk of suicide is higher for bipolar than for any other type of depression. If you think you or a friend might have bipolar disorder, seek professional help immediately.

Seasonal Affective Disorder (SAD)

People who feel unhappy during long, dark winters may have seasonal affective disorder (SAD), thought to be related to the absence of sunlight in the winter. Symptoms include:

- increased appetite
- cravings for carbohydrates

Winter's dim, cloudy days can cause people to experience physical changes that contribute to depression.

- sleeping much more than usual

- feeling irritable

- feeling like one's body is "dragging" along

The symptoms of SAD have been compared to the physical changes an animal goes through to hibernate in winter; perhaps it reflects some primitive need to shift gears and go into survival mode through the cold, dark seasons. Treatment includes light therapy to replenish the body's need for light.

Depression Related to Hormones

A small percentage of women suffer disturbing symptoms known as premenstrual dysphoric disorder (PMDD), an extreme form of the mood changes associated with the more common premenstrual mood changes. Symptoms of PMDD coincide with the menstrual cycle, with symptom-free intervals in between. These symptoms can include:

- anger

- anxiety

- bloating

- fatigue

- craving food

- feelings of guilt and self-loathing

- irritableness

- sadness

- crying

- withdrawal

Postpartum depression following childbirth might also be related to changes in female hormones, but that is not proven. This form of depression is different from postpartum "blues," which last five to ten days and go away by themselves. By contrast, postpartum depression lasts longer and requires treatment. Actress Brooke Shields helped publicize this illness following her own struggle with postpartum depression.

What Causes Depression?

You know the famous question, "Which came first, the chicken or the egg?" People cannot agree on the correct answer. Likewise, when explaining the causes of depression, scientists have gone back and forth endlessly asking, "What causes the problem—a person's physical makeup or the person's thoughts?"

The symptoms of depression have been around for as long as recorded history, and people have been trying to figure out what causes this disorder for that entire time. Scholars have regarded depression variously as a mental, spiritual, or physical problem. In the twenty-first century, experts still disagree as to causes of the illness.

There are two major theories about what causes depression: ***psychosocial*** theories and ***neurobiological*** theories. Psychosocial theories regard depression as mostly a behavioral problem. Contrasting with this view, neurobiological theories focus on the "hardware" of the mind and body; depression is viewed as genetic or physical in nature. Not surprisingly, those who focus on psychosocial theories of depression tend to favor "talk therapy" as treatment for depression. Those who favor neurobiological theories tend to focus more on drugs for treatment.

Today, most doctors and psychologists agree that the psychosocial/neurobiological issue is best answered by a "both/and" approach. Depression is a mood disorder that involves

Strategies for Coping with Depression

You can't just "snap out" of depression, but that doesn't mean you are powerless against the disease. There are ways people with depression can manage sad feelings. Treatment of depression often requires professional help, but these strategies can be used with medication or therapy to boost the healing process.

1. Get exercise.
2. Be kind to yourself; relax and pursue a favorite activity.
3. Be social; go to a fun event.
4. Eat healthy food and vitamins.
5. Talk about your feelings with friends and family.
6. Keep a "feelings journal."
7. Practice your spiritual/religious/cultural rituals.

No single treatment is the answer; usually, a combination of approaches is necessary, each playing an important role in the healing process. What's more, no two people experience depression in exactly the same way, so each person's treatment will need to be different as well.

Choosing Professional Help

The following professionals help people with depression:

- **Medical doctors (M.D.)** may prescribe antidepressants for their patients. Make sure your doctor is familiar with these medications.

- **Registered Nurses (R.N.)** can prescribe medications in some states. Make sure an R.N. is familiar with antidepressant medications.

- **Psychiatrists** are medical doctors who specialize in treating mental illness. They usually focus on prescribing medicines rather than counseling, but a few combine talk therapy with medical cures.

- **Psychologists (psychotherapists)** are professionals with a doctoral degree in psychology. They will treat depression primarily by talk therapy (counseling). Some will work in cooperation with a psychiatrist or M.D.

- **Counselors (Master of Social Work, or M.S.W.)** are similar to psychologists, but with a master's degree.

Whichever kind of caregiver you see for depression, you have the right to good treatment. It is important that you feel comfortable and confident with your mental-health provider. All conversations with these professionals are confidential; in other words, they can't tell anyone what is said to them, unless the patient gives permission or there is danger to the patient or someone else.

- A good caregiver spends time with you, asks questions, and seeks a thorough understanding of your depression.

- A good caregiver welcomes your questions.

- A good caregiver admits that she may not have all the answers for your depression and cooperates with other professionals.

- A good caregiver treats you with respect.

If you feel uncomfortable with a professional caregiver, consider switching. Do not assume you must continue with the first one assigned by your medical plan. Some doctors and psychiatrists are unsafe: be assertive in order to get the care you deserve.

the body–mind connection: *both* mind and matter contribute to the illness. Clinical psychologists Laura L. Smith and Charles H. Elliot, state, "In one sense, you can probably come to the same conclusion as the dodo bird in Alice in Wonderland and declare that 'All have won and all must have prizes.' In another sense, nobody deserves a prize . . . nobody truly knows how these factors work . . . and which ones influence other factors in various ways." For this reason, they advise, "If you encounter a professional who claims to know the single, definitive cause of depression, question that professional's

We cannot separate our minds from our bodies.

credibility. Most sophisticated experts in the field of depression know that a single, definitive cause of depression . . . likely will never be discovered." Depression is a complex interaction of experiences, coping mechanisms, temperament, biology, and genetics.

Types of Treatments

Just as many of today's professionals have come to see depression as caused by both behavioral and physical factors, they also recognize that the most effective treatments for depression involve both medicines and psychotherapy. Medication is almost always used for moderate-to-severe forms of depression, and is helpful for 60 to 80 percent of those with depression who fall in those categories. However, as Patricia Ainsworth explains in her book *Understanding Depression*, "Patients treated with a combination of antidepressant medication and psychotherapy have the best recovery rates."

Treatments for depression include the following:

- antidepressant medicines (see chapters 3 and 4)
- electroconvulsive therapy (chapter 2)
- talk therapies (chapter 2)
- natural herbal or vitamin remedies (chapter 5)
- lifestyle choices: diet, exercise, spirituality
- light therapy (for SAD)

Chapter 2

Early Concepts of Depression

Music Therapy: 1,000 BCE

A handsome young man with thick curly hair runs his fingers over the harp strings, plucking and strumming with the accomplished ease of one who has been playing an instrument as long as he can remember. Exquisite melodies vibrate from the strings and fill the air of the goatskin tent. Next to the young man, on an ornately carved ivory chair, sits an older man with long curls of gray hair, dressed in robes of fine silk. He stares off into space, a troubled furrow on his brow.

The young man pauses his playing. He gently addresses his companion, "My Lord, how are you feeling? Does this tune please you?"

The older man slowly turns to the young man beside him. He speaks slowly, as if each word must be dragged up from deep inside of his afflicted soul. "Yes, lad, I do feel . . . somewhat better." He pauses; it is evident that the harpist's gift helps him only partially. "The evil is so thick upon me. . . . My heart is filled with demons . . . yet your tunes do help somewhat. Play on, David, play on."

The book of 1 Samuel in the Hebrew Bible was written sometime between 1,000 and 600 BCE. Medical historians regard this incident, described in chapter 16, as one of the most ancient descriptions of depression, "an evil spirit from the Lord tormented him [King Saul]." It also contains an early form of therapy: "David would take his harp and play. Then relief would come to Saul and he would feel better, and the evil spirit would leave him."

The Ancient East: Herbs and Evil Spirits

The world's most ancient civilizations began in the Middle East and South Asia, so the earliest records of depression and its treatment come from ancient **Mesopotamia**, Egypt, Israel, and India. Ancient people believed depression and other mental disorders were caused by supernatural beings, so prayers, spells, and magic were used for cures. At the same time, these early civilizations recognized natural medicines—herbs and wild plants—could cure mental disorders.

In ancient Egypt, depression was described as "fever in the heart," "dryness of the heart," "falling of the heart," "debility of the heart," and "kneeling of the mind." The Egyptians blamed illnesses on Sekhmet, the lioness-goddess, who punished humanity for sins, and they worshipped Imhotep, the god of healing and medicine. One treatment for mental illnesses was sleeping overnight in a sacred temple.

Although they understood "dryness of the heart" as supernaturally caused, the ancient Egyptians developed a number of functional treatments. These included herbal medicines, massage, heliotherapy (exposure to sunlight), and hydrotherapy (water treatment). The most venerated remedy for "fever in the heart" was alcohol, noted in the Eber Papyrus of 1600

Ancient Egyptians blamed the lion-headed goddess Sekhmet for all illnesses, including depression.

BCE. Through the centuries, alcoholic beverages have been among the most common—and commonly abused—remedies for depression.

Ancient Babylonians and Assyrians also blamed supernatural beings for mental illness, and Babylonian priests diagnosed illnesses by magic. Nonetheless, the ancient Mesopotamians had a sophisticated knowledge of natural medicines. Clay tablets in the library of King Assurbanipal of Assyria (668–626 BCE) list 120 mineral medicines and 250 vegetable cures. One cure for depression was the narcotic opium, produced from poppies and known as "the plant of joy." Opium was used as an antidepressant until modern times.

Ancient India: Bhutavidya and Doshas

The Vedas, from India, are considered to be among the oldest sacred writings in the world, some dating to 3000 BCE. The Vedas include Ayurveda, a system of medicine practiced in India five thousand years ago. One of the branches of Ayurveda is Bhutavidya, or study of psychology. The word literally means "knowledge of ghosts," as they blamed evil spirits for mental illness. Treatments included herbs, diet, and yoga.

While they believed in supernatural causes, ancient Indians also had a more complex understanding of depression. The Vedas describe three doshas (air, heat, and water) that exist within each person. According to the Vedas, when these doshas are in balance, people are healthy. However, if a person's body became dominated by air, it causes depression or other mental illnesses.

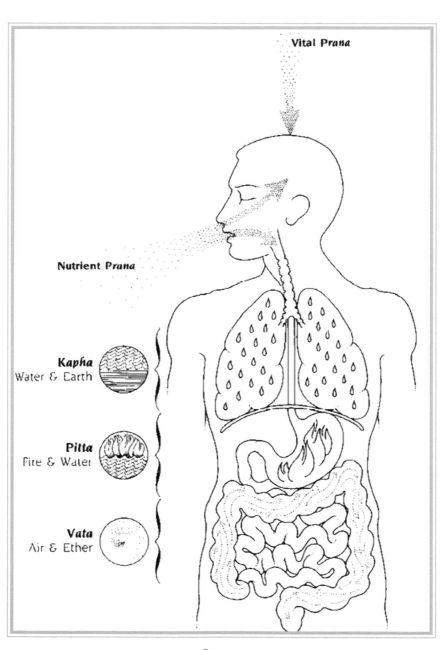

Vital Prana

Nutrient Prana

Kapha
Water & Earth

Pitta
Fire & Water

Vata
Air & Ether

Although the Ayurveda is an ancient system of medicine, people today still practice it. According to this medical perspective, depression results when a person's body is dominated by air.

*An ancient portrayal of Hippocrates, the
father of modern medicine*

Bleeding Cures

Imagine you tell your psychiatrist you are struggling with feelings of despair and unhappiness. He nods and tells you, "You have bad substances in your blood, so we will have to bleed it out of you." He ties your arm down on a table, takes out a sharp steel instrument, cuts into a vein, and allows your blood to pour into a bowl for the next half hour.

It sounds awful, but bleeding was practiced for three thousand years as a cure for depression. According to Gilbert Seigworth, "Bloodletting began with the Egyptians of the River Nile one thousand years B.C., and the tradition spread to the Greeks and Romans; its popularity continued throughout the Middle Ages. It reached its zenith during the beginning of the nineteenth century, but had virtually died as a therapeutic tool by the end of that century." Ancient bloodletting instruments included thorns, sharp pieces of flint, sharks' teeth, and leeches. Later, lancets were made of copper, iron, and steel. Bloodletting caused patients with a strong heart pulse and red skin to turn pale and cool as their bodies suffered from the loss of vital fluids; primitive doctors concluded that this represented improvement in the patients' health.

Ancient Greece: Melancholia and Humors

For more than two millennia, doctors have followed the ideas of Hippocrates, a Greek physician born in 460 BCE on the island of Cos. He is truly the father of modern medicine, because he based his medical practice on observations and study of the human body. He believed diseases were caused by

Evil Spirits in the Wilderness

Fourth-century Egyptian monks who lived in the desert wilderness coined the term acedia to describe what we now call depression. They lived lonely, austere lives, drinking only water, eating only bread, sometimes living alone in caves. They struggled at times with feelings of unhappiness or despair. These bouts of lowered emotions and physical weariness they termed "acedia" (slowness), and they regarded them as afflictions by the devil. For these desert monks, every ailment and problem was a challenge from evil spirits. So they began speaking about "the demon of acedia" that caused depression. This in turn led to the later medieval church viewing acedia as a spiritual affliction.

physical changes in the body, not by evil spirits or magic. Although that sounds obvious today, it was a vast step forward in diagnosing and treating diseases.

Hippocrates introduced the word ***melancholia*** to describe depressive illness, and the word stuck for more than two thousand years. Melancholia comes from two Greek words meaning black ***bile***. Hippocrates believed black bile was a substance in the body that caused melancholia, and that idea persisted until the eighteenth century. Hippocrates believed there were four different substances, called ***humors***, which fill each human body. These are blood, yellow bile, black bile, and phlegm. When the four humors are properly balanced, people are healthy. However, if someone's humors get out of balance, he becomes sick. Depression (melancholia) results from an overabundance of black bile.

If an imbalance of humors makes one sick, it is vital to keep them in harmony. Hippocrates taught there are six non-naturals: air, exercise, sleep, diet, urination and bowel movements, and emotions. He believed that depression and other illnesses were cured by altering a patient's use of these. Hippocrates recognized that depression was caused by physical factors and could be treated by changes in the patient's environment, assumptions still important in treating depression today.

During the Middle Ages, many illnesses were blamed on demons.

Depression in the Middle Ages: Black Bile or Deadly Sin?

A thousand years after the classical era of Greece, European tribesmen overran the Roman Empire and plunged the Western world into a time known as the Dark Ages. As Europe recovered culturally, society relied increasingly on religious faith. Therefore, spiritual beliefs dominated every area of life, including health care.

A medieval portrayal of a woman praying as she is oppressed by the seven deadly sins; during the Middle Ages, depression came to be associated with sin.

During the Middle Ages, there were two contrasting views of melancholia. Some doctors continued to follow the beliefs of the ancient Greeks. However, philosophers and theologians emphasized a religious view of depression; it was not melancholia (an illness) but *acedia* (the Latin word for laziness, sloth, or slowness)—one of the seven deadly sins defined by the Christian church.

From the thirteenth to sixteenth centuries, people suffering with depression received differing diagnosis and treatment, depending where they went for help. A priest might warn the sufferer about the sin of acedia, and urge him to attend church and pray more. Unfortunately, these cures did little to dispel the depression, and the patient now had the guilt of sin added onto feelings of despair already caused by the disease.

On the other hand, a monk might say it was a melancholic disease and prescribe herbal medicines. Monasteries quietly served as healing centers for much of Europe as monks passed down knowledge of herbs and medicinal plants from generation to generation. This included the use of **St. John's wort**, a natural remedy for depression that many people continue to rely on for treatment.

Arab Medicine in the Middle Ages

Arabic physicians in the medieval world continued the heritage of Hippocrates, regarding melancholia as an illness and refining its treatment. Though all spoke or read the Arabic language, not all of these doctors were Muslims living in the

Middle East. Some were Syrians and others were Spaniards, some were Christians and others Jews.

The most important of the medieval Arabic physicians was Ishaq Ibn Imran, a Muslim living in Baghdad in the early tenth century, who wrote a major treatise on melancholia. His description of the illness could hardly be improved on today, "an irrational, constant sadness or dejection . . . anxiety or brooding." He also correctly noted these symptoms are accompanied by "loss of weight and sleeplessness." Imran treated these symptoms with a soothing combination of

The Devil Made Her Do It: Witch Trials and Mental Disorders During the Renaissance

The Renaissance era brings to mind the great artistic achievements of Michelangelo and da Vinci, but there were dark undercurrents at this time of history. When men felt sexual temptation, they blamed evil forces for their desires. The Malleus Maleficarum, a Renaissance-era guidebook on how to spot witches, blames both lust and illnesses on witches' spells. Since these superstitions were common, people suffering from illness accused female neighbors of practicing black magic, and these alleged witches were tortured and often burned alive. Many victims of the witch hunts were women suffering from mental illnesses.

During the Renaissance, people believed in witchcraft, and suspected witches were often put to death. Here, a witch is portrayed flying on the back of a goat.

Lincoln's Depression

Most of us think of Abraham Lincoln as a great and strong leader, the president who ended slavery and kept the United States together. Many of us, however, don't know about his lifelong struggle with depression. Several times in his life, Lincoln became so depressed he spoke seriously of suicide. When Lincoln was a young man in Salem, Illinois, friends kept watch over him when he was so depressed he couldn't get out of bed; those who knew him then said they had never seen a more despairing person. Lincoln's suffering helped mold him into the extraordinarily wise and compassionate leader needed by a nation in crisis; he escaped the pain of his depression by focusing on doing his best for his country.

therapies: carefully chosen diet, massages, moderate exercise, sympathetic discussions, and music.

The Age of Reason

The seventeenth and eighteenth centuries in Europe are known as the Enlightenment or the Age of Reason, an era dominated by belief in **rationality**. During this time, philosophers and physicians began to rethink the assumptions of ancient Greeks and medieval churchmen regarding depression. Talk of witchcraft was dispelled by scientific observations of illnesses and the human body.

French philosopher René Descartes (1596–1650) suggested melancholia originated at the place where the human soul and body connected. He said this was the brain, specifically the ***pineal gland***. This was a bold move, because for thousands of years following Hippocrates, physicians had assumed depression originated with black bile in the liver or heart. Descartes moved the search for depression's origin in the right direction.

Samuel Johnson (1709–1784) is the most quoted English writer after Shakespeare; he also changed the way people talk about melancholia/depression. Johnson struggled at times with major depression, describing it as "a dejection, gloom,

In the eighteenth century, Samuel Johnson helped coin the word "depression."

and despair which made existence misery." While this influential writer sometimes used "melancholia" to describe his illness, he often spoke of it as "depression," from the Latin term "pressed down." If not for this great writer, we might still be speaking of "melancholia."

The Birth of Psychology

It was the dawn of a new century and a new way of thinking. A young woman, dressed in layers of fashionable and uncom-

Patent Medications and High Times in the Late 1800s

In America and Canada in the late nineteenth and early twentieth centuries, most people saved money by tending to their own medical needs, rather than seeing a doctor. Medications were so-called "patent medicines." Although many of these remedies were actually patented, others were simply home concoctions placed in bottles with distinctive labels. Patent medicines were big business: by 1900, there were more than a million on the market. Most claimed to cure scores of different illnesses, including depression. Common "active ingredients" were the narcotic opium or high percentages of alcohol. Not surprisingly, many consumers attested that patent medicines made them feel better. One patent medicine was called "Soothing Baby Syrup" and claimed to stop babies from crying. It contained opium and really worked: unfortunately, it turned babies into addicts.

fortable Victorian clothing, reclines on a fainting couch, her mouth moving slowly and tears in the corners of her eyes. A sharply dressed man with mustache and goatee sits in a chair on the other side of the room, asking occasional questions and furiously scribbling down all the young woman's remarks. The year is 1899, the city is Vienna, and although this scene hardly seems dramatic, Sigmund Freud is about to change forever the ways the world understands mental illness. Sigmund Freud (1856–1939) is known as the father of psychoanalysis and recognized as one of the most influential thinkers of the twentieth century. However, before looking at Freud's contributions, one needs to consider how a contemporary of his influenced our understanding of depression.

German psychologist Emil Kraepelin (1856–1926) played a vital role in categorizing the forms of depressive illnesses. He tried to treat severe depression with hypnosis, opium, and morphine, but was frustrated that only a third of his patients improved. Kraepelin noticed that certain patients changed moods, at times talking excitedly and appearing unaware of their limitations. He coined the phrase "manic-depressive disorder," what is now called bipolar disorder. He also noted some cases that he termed *endogenous* depression, illnesses seemingly arising from within the patient, while other cases were classified as reactive depression, ones obviously caused by crises in the patient's life. The terms have all changed, but Kraepelin defined the modern categories of major depression, bipolar disorder, and adjustment disorder with depressed mood. This careful explanation of different forms of depression with distinctive symptoms was a milestone in treating these illnesses.

Sigmund Freud pioneered the principles of modern psychology. He established the idea of the talking cure, or psychotherapy—treatment of mental disorders by helping patients investigate their lives. He also suggested the idea of the unconscious mind—that people are to a large extent unaware of the processes going on in their brains, processes that can cause or cure mental illness. This was a revolutionary idea, since people had always before considered that behavior and thoughts were things over which they had no control

Emil Kraepelin

Sigmund Freud, the father of modern psychology

(rather than things that could be investigated, explored, and changed).

Regarding depression, Freud noticed the similarity between symptoms of grief and those of depression, leading him to suggest depression is caused by a significant loss in the patient's life. Later, he suggested that depression is caused by sexual desires a patient cannot satisfy. The struggle between sexual desire and morality takes place in the unconscious mind, so it is unrecognized by the patient even while it hurts him. Few of today's psychologists follow Freud's beliefs about the sexual causes of depression, though some still believe depression may be caused by an unconscious sense of loss.

Psychosocial Treatments for Depression Today

Until the 1970s, the talking cure was the standard treatment method for depression; antidepressants have since taken over as the most common form of treatment. Nonetheless, many health-care professionals consider the combination of both medication and psychotherapy as the ideal treatment.

Psychodynamic therapy is an offspring of Freud's technique. This approach assumes that a patient suffers depression due to unconscious desires and conflicts. Suppose a hypothetical patient—Jim—goes to see a psychologist who uses this technique. Jim is suffering a bout of major depression, feeling tired, losing appetite, and feeling unhappy and desperate much of the time, though he doesn't know why. The therapist asks Jim to talk about his past, especially his childhood and relationships with his parents. As they talk, Jim realizes that his father neglected him and criticized him frequently during his childhood. Jim is surprised at the unhappiness that comes over him as he discusses these things. He realized that patterns of feelings and behaviors exist, connecting past experiences and relationships to his present life. This breakthrough understanding about how he missed his father's love enables Jim to recover, over time, from his depression.

Interpersonal therapy assumes depression is caused by the frustrations of everyday life, mostly those dealing with relationships. People form good or bad feelings about themselves based on the ways other people treat them; the best way to improve self-concept and feel better is to improve people skills, thereby enabling better relationships.

Psychoanalytic analysis looks at early parent–child interactions as the source of adult depression and anxiety.

Suppose Jim goes to see an interpersonal therapist with the same set of symptoms. This therapist isn't much concerned with Jim's childhood. She wants to know all about Jim's life today, including his relationships with his wife, children,

According to cognitive therapy, we do not have to passively accept the thoughts that enter our minds; instead, we can choose to think only positive thoughts.

golf partners, coworkers, and so on. Through a number of conversations, Jim realizes that he feels inferior to some of his coworkers, who close more sales than he does and sometimes mistreat him. As they continue meeting, the therapist "coaches" Jim on ways to talk more effectively with his coworkers. Over time, he feels surer about himself and the depression gradually lifts.

Cognitive therapy is based on the idea that "we are what we think." It doesn't matter so much what happens to people, either in the past or the present; instead, it is the way they process those events that makes them depressed. Automatic, negative thoughts tend to pervasive when a person is depressed—but those thoughts can be changed.

Jim sees a cognitive therapist and they talk about Jim's life, both past and present. The therapist helps Jim see that he is playing out negative predictions, expecting the worst and then sometimes making that happen. The therapist helps Jim understand how unrealistic assumptions make him unhappy: he is a perfectionist and would be happier if he accepted that he can't always be outstanding or flawless. The therapist also helps Jim to be more aware of his emotions and what they are telling him. All of this enables Jim to dialogue with himself and stop thoughts that make him unhappy. Though his outward circumstances haven't changed much, *he* has.

Today, many psychotherapists combine these approaches and use different forms of therapy according to the different needs of each client.

Electroconvulsive Therapy (ECT)

It was January 24, 1934, in a mental hospital at Lipotmezö, Hungary. A thirty-year-old man named Zoltan lay motionless on his bed. For four years, he had hardly spoken. Zoltan suffered from acute schizophrenia, and at this time, his case was considered hopeless. Psychiatrist Ladislas Meduna approached the bed with a hypodermic needle and injected camphor into the patient. Before long, Zoltan began jerking wildly and rolled off the bed. He was the first patient in history to go through an artificially induced grand mal seizure. As far back as the ancient Greeks, doctors had noticed that patients who

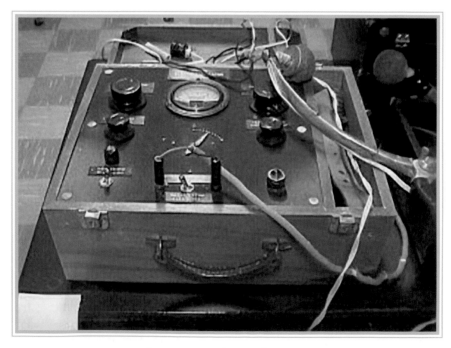

*A device used to administer
electroconvulsive therapy in the 1940s*

suffered from epileptic seizures seemed to recover from other ill-nesses after their convulsions. Now, Dr. Meduna was attempting to produce the same results with an artificial seizure. He repeated the process four more times. After the fifth seizure, the hoped-for cure occurred. Zoltan got out of bed and asked for breakfast. He could not believe that he had been in the hospital for the past four years. He was healed of the "incurable" schizophre-nia and could live on his own and succeed at a job.

Dr. Meduna repeated the process with other schizophrenic patients, achieving the same results. However, it was danger-ous using chemicals to produce the seizure. In 1938, Italians Ugo Cerletti and Luigi Bini induced seizures using electric-ity. The seizure was immediate and just as effective as those induced by *intravenous* chemicals, but the violence of the seizures caused harm to some patients, so the doctors injected muscle relaxants into the patients before the shock treat-ments. This was the beginning of modern electroconvulsive therapy, also called ECT.

ECT was widely used until the 1970s, when antidepres-sants became popular and the movie *One Flew Over the Cuck-oo's Nest* caused the public to disfavor electroshock treatment. Through the 1980s and 1990s, it appeared ECT would fade into history, but it did not do so. In the early years of the twenty-first century, ECT is again a treatment method for se-vere depression. Because insurance companies prefer not to pay for lengthy hospital stays, and ECT treatments often work more quickly than antidepressants in treatment of severe de-pression, ECT is increasing as a favored hospital treatment.

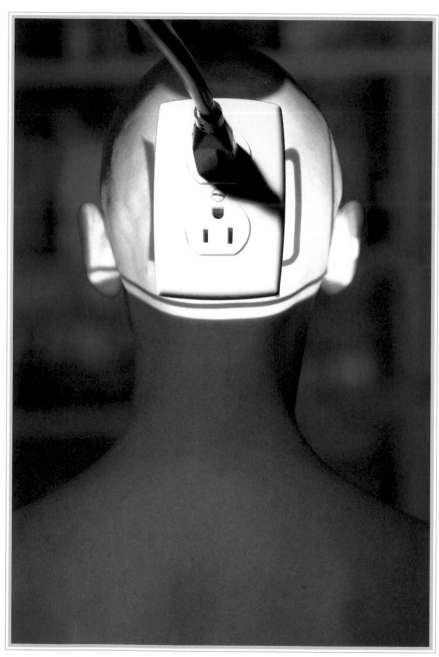

Although many researchers believe ECT is safe and effective, many people are horrified by the idea of "plugging in" the brain to an electrical current.

Every year, between 100,000 and 150,000 patients in the United States receive ECT.

How is it that grand mal seizures, similar to those experienced in epilepsy, can remove symptoms of depression? Psychiatrist Max Fink, a pioneer in the use of ECT, admits in a recent article, "For the moment scientists have no answer to this question—we simply don't understand how ECT has the restorative capacity that it does."

An American Psychiatric Association report says that ECT has an 80 percent success rate, higher than most antidepressants. They say it is "often the safest, fastest and most effective treatment." After sixty years of use, there is no study that proves brain damage due to ECT. ECT has proven effective in treating some patients whose depression did not respond either to psychotherapy or antidepressants, and some patients attest they would probably have committed suicide if not for help they received from ECT treatments.

At the same time, there is a vocal community who oppose ECT. They point to the side effect of memory loss. This is usually short in duration, but some patients report memory loss covering much longer spans of time. Psychiatrist Peter Breggin says shock treatment is "like playing Russian roulette with your brain." John Breeding, a psychologist with over twenty years of professional practice, testified before a New York State committee reviewing ECT, saying, "I am convinced that electroshock is dangerous, harmful, and unnecessary." ECT continues to be controversial; people have strong emotional arguments for or against the practice.

Chapter 3

Breakthroughs in Medicine

"**I** felt like 60, now I feel like 15. I can't get depressed anymore even when I try. I get a zest out of such common things as drinking coffee, breathing fresh air." This quote appears in "A New Wonder Drug for Depression," a 1957 article in *Better Homes and Gardens*. It describes the effects of a then newly discovered "psychic energizer," iproniazid (iproniazid phosphate, originally marketed with the brand name Marsilid), one of the first prescription antidepressants. While the article reflects public enthusiasm for this scientific breakthrough, its timing is sadly ironic. Shortly after its publication, the new drug was removed from the market as more than a hundred patients taking the drug developed

Scientists sometimes stumble on new cures while they're in the midst of researching another condition.

serious liver problems. This account shows that the invention and development of antidepressant drugs was not always simple or straightforward.

Accidental Discoveries: Monoamine Oxidase Inhibitors and Tricyclics

Major advances in science sometimes come about by "accidental" means: a researcher intending a certain kind of result from an experiment discovers something that is entirely different yet useful for humanity. The classic example is Sir Alexander Fleming's observation of a bacterial culture in his laboratory that was accidentally contaminated by a mold, leading to the discovery of penicillin.

The first breakthroughs in antidepressant medications occurred in a similar manner. In the 1950s, doctors were researching a medicine, iproniazid, hoping it would treat tuberculosis. The medicine proved ineffective in treating tuberculosis, but researchers noticed patients who had been suffering from depressed moods were emotionally elevated. Based on this, the doctors decided to try a related experiment. Reserpine was a medicine used to lower blood pressure, and it had the unfortunate side effect of causing depression in patients. Researchers gave iproniazid to patients who were taking reserpine; if their hypothesis was correct, patients taking both reserpine and iproniazid would experience less depression than those who took only reserpine. Results proved this hypothesis correct and confirmed that iproniazid worked as an antidepressant. Iproniazid was the first drug discovered in a family of drugs known as monoamine oxidase inhibitors (MAOIs).

Around the same time, another medicine, imipramine (later marketed as Tofranil) was used in experiments related to schizophrenia. Researchers hoped that imipramine would treat schizophrenic **psychosis**. Once again, discovery came

A person with schizophrenia has perceptions that cause him to split from reality.

Meet the Family: MAOIs

Brand Name	Generic Name
Nardil	phenelzine sulfate
Parnate	tranylcypromine sulfate

Note: MAOIs should not be taken with certain foods, including sausages, beer, red wine, avocados, aged cheese, and smoked fish, as severe reactions can occur.

Meet the Family: Tricyclics

Brand Name	Generic Name
Anafranil	clomipramine hydrochloride
Pamelor	nortriptyline hydrochloride
Sinequan	doxepin hydrochloride
Surmontil	trimipramine maleate
Tofranil	imipramine hydrochloride
Vivactil	protriptyline hydrochloride

Note: Some tricyclics can be fatal in overdoses. Prescription drugs should be taken only as prescribed by one's physician.

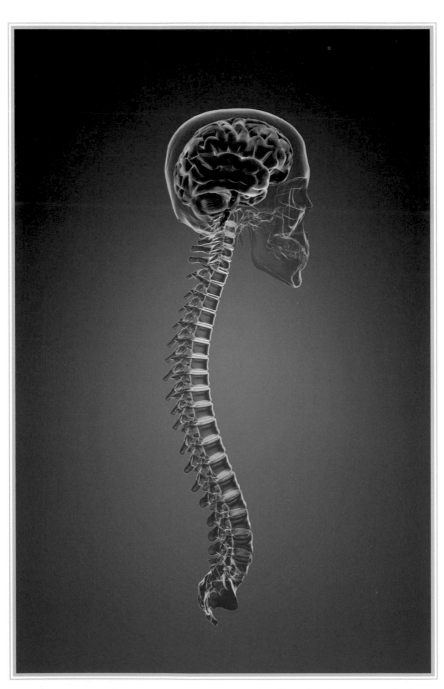

The central nervous system includes the brain and the spinal cord, as well as all the body's other nerves.

through accident. While iproniazid did not have the hoped-for effect on psychosis, it did make patients feel happier. Like researchers working with iproniazid, those developing imipramine switched to experiments directly relating to depression and found that imipramine was an antidepressant. Imipramine was the forerunner of a new class of drugs known as tricyclics, due to their molecular structure that involves three interconnected benzene rings.

Thinking About Gray Matter

How do antidepressant medications work? Although no one is completely certain about the causes of depression, researchers know it has something to do with neurons and neurotransmitters. The following is a simple explanation of how these work and what might go wrong with them. (Keep in mind, though, that doctors study for years to try to understand the brain—and yet there is still much they don't know.)

The body communicates through the central nervous system (CNS) that includes the brain, spinal cord, and peripheral nervous system (PNS) containing nerves that carry communications between the brain and the rest of the body. Antidepressants work mostly on the CNS.

The brain contains 100 billion neurons (more or less). Neurons are the primary components of the CNS, controlling actions, thoughts, and emotions. To undertake any thought or activity requires that a vast number of neurons send messages to one another. There are approximately 100 trillion different lines of communication in the nervous system. In such a huge system, things sometimes go wrong, and most experts agree depression is caused by problems in communication between neurons.

When a neuron needs to communicate with another neuron, it sends a jolt of energy down a tube called an axon. When this impulse reaches the end of the axon, the axon emits chemical messengers called neurotransmitters. Because the axons don't touch each other, the neurotransmitters float in the synapse, the space between sending and receiving neurons. Sending neurons monitor the amount of neurotransmitters they release, and sometimes reuptake chemicals that are floating in the synapse in order to keep an adequate chemical supply. Other neurotransmitters are picked up by the dendrite (intake section) of a receiving neuron and passed on down the nervous system to accomplish their task of communication.

Many researchers believe depression occurs when something goes wrong with the transmission of neurotransmitters. While there is uncertainty on the exact ways this occurs, depression appears to be related to three different neurotransmitters. These are:

- serotonin, which influences mood
- dopamine, which influences attention, motivation, and experience of pleasure
- norepinephrine (noradrenaline), which influences energy and alertness

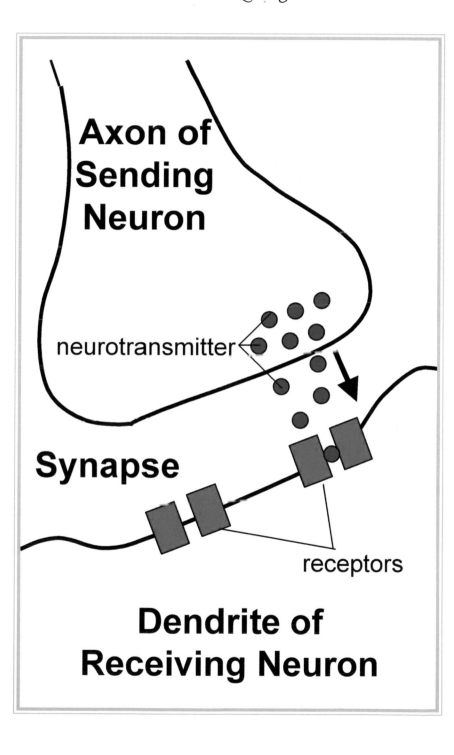

Wonder Drugs Not So Wonderful

In the early 1960s, excitement about MAOIs was diminished when some patients taking these antidepressants died from brain hemorrhages and others experienced severe headaches. These problems were the result of high blood pressure, and that was odd because MAOIs had been previously proven to *lower* blood pressure. A British pharmacist made the observation that his wife suffered similar headaches when she ate cheese, and he wrote a note to a doctor named Barry Blackwell. Blackwell in turn noted that a number of his patients were experiencing headaches after eating cheese. Blackwell discovered that aged cheese contains large amounts of a chemical that causes nerve cells to release other chemicals.

Cheese and MAOIs are a potentially deadly combination.

The combination of a MAOI plus cheese (or other foods that contain the same chemical) raised blood pressure. Physicians could still prescribe these antidepressants and warn patients away from foods that would cause the reaction, but patients who are already depressed have trouble dealing with such restrictions. Due to their potentially lethal side effects, early MAOIs fell out of favor with doctors.

Imipramine and other tricyclics also had problems. Imipramine is a "dirty" drug, meaning that it influences not only the target neurotransmitters, but a wide range of neurotransmitter functions. While patients appreciated the improvement in mood, they did not care for constipation, dry mouth, difficulty urinating, and other unpleasant side effects. What's worse, both tricyclics and MAOIs are lethal in an overdose.

An Elusive Market

Even without the unpleasant side effects, early antidepressants faced obstacles before they could achieve popularity: drug companies and physicians were unenthusiastic. Drug companies lacked a way to market the new drugs and didn't want to invest in them. Furthermore, in the 1950s, many physicians were still unaware of the prevalence of depressive illnesses. That changed with the publication of a statement by the World Health Organization (WHO) that "at least one hundred million people in the world" suffer from depression; that got the attention of pharmaceutical manufacturers.

Public attitudes toward depression also limited the market for antidepressants. Depression (along with mental health

Until recently, a depressed person was often viewed
as a possibly sinful person with moral issues.

problems in general) faced a major ***stigma***; it was as psychiatrist Nathan Kline wrote in 1964, "not fashionable to be depressed." Many people had misconceptions about depression, believing it was usually a temporary problem and people could just "snap out of it" if they chose to do so. Depression and other mental disorders were often viewed as character or moral problems, rather than medical or biological issues. In such an environment, there was little encouragement for those suffering from depression to spend their hard-earned dollars on drug treatments.

However, the world was changing. As scientists and doctors learned more about depression, they began to realize the need for a wider arsenal of treatments. Until the mid-1970s, ECT was the treatment of choice for severe depression, but when public attitudes toward it changed, fewer doctors were willing to prescribe its use. By the 1980s, the public and pharmaceutical companies were both eager to find an affective antidepressant but without the problems associated with MAOIs and tricyclics. Prozac came into the world at an opportune time.

Fresher!
Cleaner!
NEW IMPROVED LIFE!
Better
Than Ever!
#1
Prozac
MOOD BRIGHTENER
Wash Your Blues Away!

Chapter 4

Prozac Revolution

For a number of years, Rosa felt her life was under some strange curse. It's not that everything was terrible, but she didn't feel really good about anything either. She didn't care for her looks and felt uncomfortable in social situations. She did well in both high school and college academics, but after college she had trouble advancing in jobs; she was smart and competent, but too full of self-doubt to get promotions. Rosa finally decided to see a psychologist, who after a number of sessions suggested she see her doctor and ask about a prescription for Prozac (fluoxetine). After six weeks taking the drug, Rosa was astonished at the difference in her life. For the first time in half a decade, she really felt happy. She felt comfortable with her looks, was more relaxed around people, and was even promoted to manager at her job.

Prozac's birth revolutionized the way we look at depression.

She told a friend that socially, emotionally, and even spiritually she felt "like a brand-new person."

Though not everyone is as enthused as Rosa about that drug, the selective serotonin reuptake inhibitors (SSRIs), of which Prozac is one, has been the most popular set of antidepressants. Worldwide, more than 35 million people have taken Prozac, and millions more have taken other SSRIs.

Prozac Is Born

As described in the previous chapter, two families of antidepressant drugs had been developed in the 1950s, but unpleasant side effects hampered their use. At the same time, medical researchers were focusing their interest on serotonin, one of the brain's neurotransmitters. In Edinburgh, Scotland, in 1953, John Gaddum, a pioneer in *psychopharmacology*, suggested that serotonin "plays an essential part in keeping us sane." His direction led a number of researchers both in Britain and the United States to concentrate their studies on serotonin. In the late 1950s, researchers at the National Institutes of Health in Bethesda, Maryland, demonstrated that altering levels of serotonin did produce behavioral changes.

These early experiments with serotonin led Ray Fuller, the senior pharmacologist at Eli Lilly Company in Indianapolis, to push his company to research serotonin as a key to treating depression. Together with another researcher, David Wong, Fuller influenced company executives to organize a team to study the connection between serotonin and depression. Lilly Company chemist Bryan Molloy produced groups of chemicals that could serve as antidepressants without the potential side effects of MAOIs and tricyclics. These drugs limited the amount of serotonin neurons retook after releasing the chemical into the synapse, hence the name serotonin reuptake inhibitors; they allowed more serotonin to stay in the synapse and be available as a messenger. By 1974, Eli Lilly was working on a drug generically named fluoxetine, what

Questioning the Research

Before any drug can be prescribed legally in the United States it must be approved by the Food and Drug Administration, a process that takes a long time and very thorough testing. Prozac took more than a decade to move from early experiments in the 1970s to approval in 1987. Nonetheless, some critics have suggested the Eli Lilly Company manipulated results of their studies to gain FDA approval.

Psychiatrist Peter Breggin believes depression is caused entirely by psychosocial factors and therefore Prozac (and other antidepressants) fail to address the "real" causes of depression. Breggin's beliefs have led him to critically review the process that led to approval of Prozac. He claims Prozac worked little better than the placebo used in testing (a placebo is an inactive pill, a "sugar pill," given to some patients in a study; patients do not know whether they are taking the sugar pill or actual medicine). He concludes that Prozac "works" mostly in the sense that patients expect it to work.

Some critics suggest that sugar pills would
have as much effect as Prozac.

Prozac appeared to be the perfect antidepressant.

would later be given the trade name Prozac. Testing of the drug with volunteers began in 1976.

Encouraged by the early results of their research, in 1980 Lilly hired an independent researcher to do more work and hopefully prove the value of fluoxetine. Psychiatrist John Feighner of La Mesa, California, helped test the drug. By 1983, Feighner delivered even better news than the Lilly team had hoped for. Fluoxetine worked as well as other antidepressants, but it did not have the nasty side effects. Furthermore, there was an added bonus: Feighner observed that fluoxetine caused weight loss, in contrast with other antidepressants that caused weight gain. In its 1985 annual report, the Lilly Company mentioned fluoxetine as a weight-loss drug under development, and investment in the company jumped as a result. Testing fluoxetine went on for two more years with even more positive results of its *efficacy* as an antidepressant. As a result, Lilly dropped the idea of marketing the new drug as a weight-loss medication, pitching it as an antidepressant instead.

In December 1987, the Food and Drug Administration (FDA) approved Prozac (the trade name for fluoxetine) for use as an antidepressant. Its success in terms of sales was phenomenal; for better or worse, the Prozac revolution had begun.

Prozac Gets Rave Reviews

In a 1989 *New York* magazine article, journalist Fran Schumer reported, "Less than two years after Eli Lilly and Company put

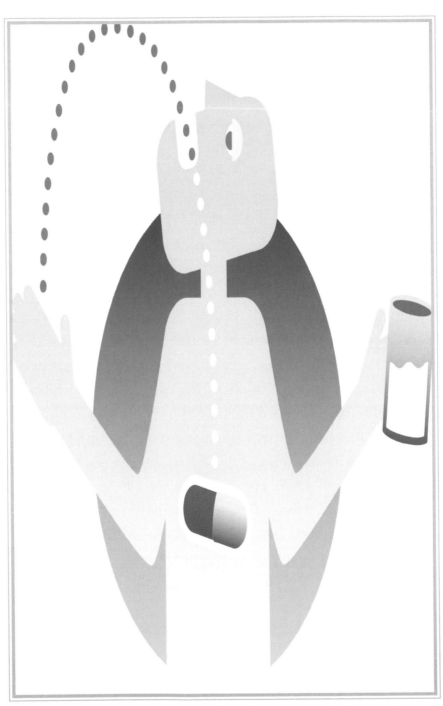

By the 1990s, Prozac was a familiar household product.

it on the market, fluoxetine hydrochloride (Prozac's chemical name) is the antidepressant most widely prescribed in the United States." She describes a patient, Rachel, who told her psychiatrist "we should all go out and buy Eli Lilly stock." Her psychiatrist responded, "You're too late." Within only a couple of years from hitting the market, Prozac was already on its way toward a billion dollars in sales.

At the time Prozac was introduced, the American public had become more aware of depressive illnesses, and there were fewer stigmas in taking antidepressant medications. ECT had fallen into disfavor, and the side effects of MAOIs and tricyclics were well known. The world was ready for a safe antidepressant, and, therefore, Prozac sold more quickly than any psychiatric drug in history. By 1990, three years after its release, it was the number-one drug prescribed by psychiatrists. In a 1990 article, the *New York Times* declared "With millions taking Prozac, a legal drug culture arises." In 1994, *Newsweek* said, "Prozac has attained the familiarity of Kleenex and the legal status of spring water. The Drug has shattered old stigmas." By that year, Prozac had become the second-best-selling drug in the entire world (the leading drug was an ulcer treatment named Zantac).

Prozac Influences Public Ideas About Mental Health

While the medical market in 1987 fueled the success of Prozac, the success of Prozac in turn influenced the drug market and public perceptions of depression itself. *Newsweek* in 1990 noted, "As Prozac's success stories mount, so does the sense that depression and other mental disorders are just that— treatable illnesses, not failings of character." For centuries, science had argued whether depression was an illness caused

Meet the Family: Selective Serotonin Reuptake Inhibitors (SSRIs)

Brand Name	Generic Name
Celexa	citalopram hydrobromide
Lexapro	escitalopram oxalate
Paxil	paroxetine hydrochloride
Prozac	fluoxetine hydrochloride
Zoloft	sertraline hydrochloride

Note: SSRIs can be dangerous for patients with bipolar disorder and can cause dangerous reactions if taken with antidepressants in the MAOI family. In 2005, the FDA issued two warnings concerning Paxil; one cited the drug as a possible cause of suicide in children and the other warned of the danger of birth defects when taken by pregnant women.

*Prozac convinced people that depression was a
treatable illness rather than a character failing.*

by psychosocial factors or biological factors; the apparent success of Prozac in treating millions of people lent validity to the idea that depression was indeed a biological illness (or at least it had a biological component).

By the mid-1990s, Prozac became so acceptable that some people *wanted* to take it even if they were not clinically depressed. Officials at the Lilly Company were concerned about misuse of their product. In 1993, Dr. Gary Tollefson, a researcher for Lilly, explained, "We don't want people to confuse someone with a serious medical problem with someone

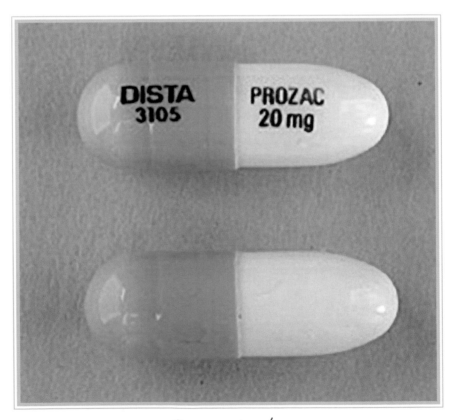

Prozac capsules

who has one or two 'down' days. We don't want everyone lumped together."

Most psychiatrists today continue to use SSRIs as standard treatments for depression. However, they are not miracle drugs. In the early years of the twenty-first century, debate rages over Prozac's merits. There are still many satisfied customers, yet others challenge its effectiveness and its safety.

Chapter 5

Controversies and Alternatives

*T*wo Hollywood lives, associated with humor and beauty, ended in murder and suicide. According to lawyers, however, the real culprit was antidepressant medication. Phil Hartman was a nationally known comedian, famous for his roles on *Saturday Night Live*, from 1987 to 1994. He also starred in the sitcom *NewsRadio* and did voices for *The Simpsons*. In 1986, Hartman married a former model, Brynn. They had two children and appeared to have a perfect life at their Encino, California, home. However, close friends of the couple knew their lives were less happy than they appeared to be. Brynn struggled with depression,

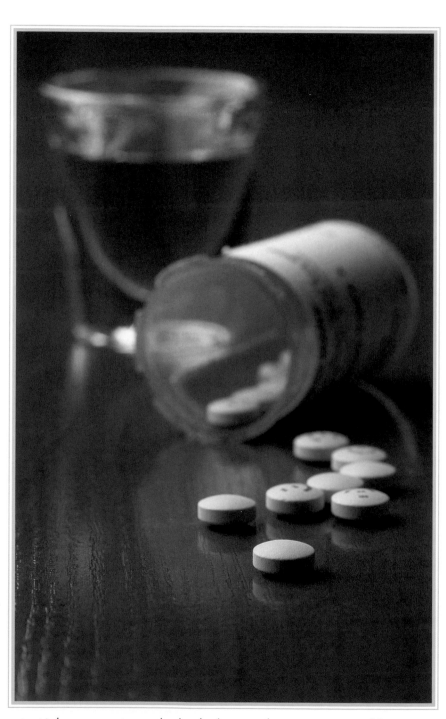

Antidepressants and alcohol are a dangerous combination.

and her physician prescribed Zoloft (sertraline, an antidepressant medicine in the SSRI family) for treatment. According to press accounts, she also sought relief by drinking and using illegal drugs, and their marriage unraveled as a result.

On the night of May 28, 1998, this Hollywood romance turned to tragedy. Phil Hartman threatened to leave his wife if she did not turn her life around. Seeking solace, she spent the night drinking

Safety Tips for Antidepressant Medications

Antidepressants are powerful drugs with possibly serious side effects. If you take one, you should follow these tips for safety and effectiveness.

• *Tell your doctor about all other physical conditions you have before she prescribes antidepressant medication (especially if you are pregnant).*

• *Tell your doctor all other medications you take, including nonprescription "natural" remedies (some of these react dangerously with prescription antidepressants).*

• *Tell your doctor about any side effects you experience while taking antidepressants.*

• *Never mix alcohol or street drugs with prescription medications.*

• *Don't hesitate to talk with your doctor about any concerns; your health is important, and you should insist on being taken seriously.*

at a local restaurant. She returned home in the early morning, took out a pistol she had purchased for personal protection, shot and killed her husband. She went to a friend's house and confessed her crime, and the friend called the police. As the police arrived, Brynn shot herself; authorities found the couple's two children, physically unharmed, in the house.

This would be just another lurid story in the annals of celebrity murder cases except for what happened afterward. The **executor** of Hartman's estate, Brynn Hartman's brother, filed a wrongful death suit against Pfizer Inc., the manufacturer of Zoloft. The suit alleged that Pfizer did not properly report the drug's potential side effects to the public. "Zoloft is an antidepressant that in some people causes violent and suicidal side effects," said an attorney representing the Hartman estate. The case was complicated because Mrs. Hartman had not only taken her prescribed dosage of Zoloft the night of the murder, an autopsy found cocaine and alcohol in her blood as well. Was Zoloft to blame for the murder-suicide, or did intoxication and a troubled emotional state lead to the deaths? After several years, Pfizer settled with the Hartman estate for an undisclosed amount of money.

Second Thoughts About Antidepressant Medicines

The Hartman tragedy may be the most dramatic case involving the dangerous side effect of an antidepressant medicine, but it is by no means the only one. Public opinion tends to swing from one extreme to the other, and the nearly unanimous reports that SSRIs were a "wonder medicine" in the early 1990s changed to controversies and complaints about the medications by the middle of the same decade.

In July of 1990, a forty-year-old woman sued Eli Lilly and company, claiming Prozac caused her to attempt suicide. Television stations showed pictures of the claimant with scars where she had slashed herself. Immediately, hundreds

Phil and Brynn Hartman

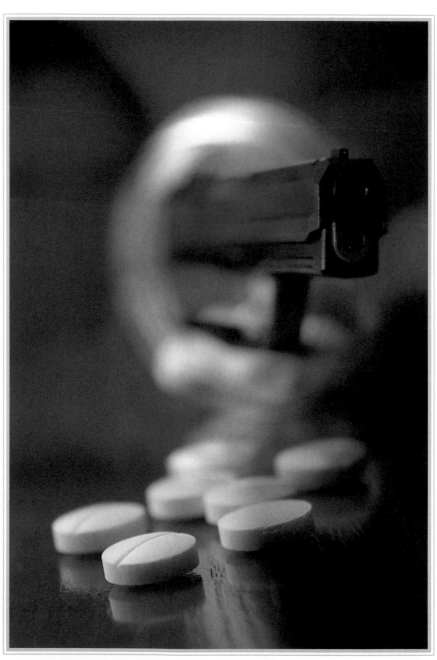

It's difficult to connect Prozac to violence and suicide, since people were committing suicide and murder long before Prozac came along.

of people called their lawyers, wanting to sue for alleged harm done by Prozac. Some had injured themselves, others had attempted suicide, and others were family members of those who had succeeded in committing suicide. The week after the woman's lawsuit became public, three families of murder victims launched another suit. They claimed a Louisville, Kentucky, man who killed eight victims with a shotgun did so because he was taking Prozac.

Such allegations are difficult to prove. As medicine reporter Denise Grady wrote in 1990, "Given that 30,000 Americans a year were killing themselves before Prozac came along, it may be hard to prove that patients became suicidal from Prozac and not from depression itself." Indeed, Eli Lilly pointed out that depressed patients were twenty-two to thirty-six times more likely than the general public to commit suicide. No drug is perfect, and studies show Prozac is helpful only to approximately 60 percent of patients, and it may take up to eight weeks to begin working.

The allegations of Prozac's harmfulness that arose in the early 1990s did not succeed in pinning blame on the manufacturer: Eli Lilly settled cases out of court or got charges dismissed. However, at the end of the decade, a new set of challenges arose. The Hartman case and a school slaying put antidepressants back into the headlines. After the frenzy of death and destruction at Columbine High in Littleton, Colorado, newspapers reported that one of the killers, Eric Harris, was taking Luxov® (fluvoxamine maleate, a drug in the SSRI family) at the time he committed the murders. However, these cases were again inconclusive. The Columbine shootings had been deliberately and methodically planned out months in advance; blaming the massacre on a medicine failed to explain adequately the Columbine killings. Likewise, Brynn Hartman's night of murder and suicide could be blamed on cocaine and alcohol as much as on Zoloft.

In the early twenty-first century, a new round of antidepressant concerns gained public notice. In July of 2005, the FDA issued a public health advisory related to antidepressants. The advisory was issued in "response to recent scientific publications that report the possibility of increased risk of suicidal behavior in adults treated with antidepressants." It included advice that "Adults whose symptoms worsen while being treated with antidepressants, including an increase in suicidal thinking or behavior, should be evaluated by their health care professional."

At the same time, another FDA document warned about antidepressants prescribed for children and adolescents. Many antidepressant prescription drugs developed for adults are regularly prescribed to young persons even though they have never been specifically approved for use by children and adolescents. Children and adolescents make up about 8 percent of patients receiving antidepressant drugs in the United States, over ten million prescriptions for patients under age eighteen in 2003. A January 2005 FDA document titled "Suicidality in Children and Adolescents," reported a study of nine antidepressant medications, including SSRIs, found that child and teen patients with major depressive disorder

Incidents of school violence have been
blamed on antidepressant use, but again,
the facts are difficult to prove.

Do antidepressants offer more good than evil? Or are their side effects so dangerous that they outweigh their benefits?

(twenty-four clinical trials with 4,400 patients) revealed a greater risk of "suicidal behavior or thinking (suicidality)" during the first few months of patients receiving antidepressants.

In January of 2006, a pair of federally funded studies supported the safety of antidepressant medications. The first study surveyed three thousand adults and found that half experienced some improvement from major depression after taking antidepressant medications. The second study of 65,000 adults and teens affirmed that antidepressant medications lessened the likelihood of suicide in patients with depression.

Controversy over the use of antidepressants continues. Critics insist antidepressant medications do little to help patients, and may actually cause them harm. Many doctors and psychiatrists respond that antidepressants prevent suicides because patients improve with the medications. Thus the merits of antidepressant medications are hotly debated.

Natural Remedies for Depression

Considering the bad press and FDA warnings surrounding prescription antidepressants, it is not surprising that many who suffer from depression turn to natural remedies. These are "natural" as they are produced or extracted from herbs and other plants. A study published in the February 2001 edition of *the American Journal of Psychiatry* reported a study showing that more than half of those who suffer from severe depression take some form of natural therapy.

Critics point out that most natural treatments for depression are not approved by the FDA. Furthermore, there is no official regulation of natural medications, so a consumer cannot be certain of the purity of the natural remedies she purchases. However, advocates for natural remedies claim that FDA testing is expensive and time consuming, so herbal remedies are unlikely to ever be tested and approved in a manner similar to pharmaceutical drugs. More than 120 pharmaceutical medicines on the market today are plant-derived, and scientists continue to research plants as a source of chemicals that may provide significant cures for disease, so advocates of natural remedies believe they may be ahead of officially approved medicines. Plants contain amazingly complex combinations of various chemicals, in opposition to medicines that usually contain fewer chemical components, and natural health experts claim nature's bewildering complexity provides beneficial results that are almost impossible to reproduce by artificial means.

A **veritable** ocean of Internet sites, books, and magazines tout the effectiveness of natural remedies, and natural medicines are an enormous industry. Again, critics emphasize that there is little regulation for these claims; consumers are taking a leap of faith. On the other hand, advocates of natural medications point out that even FDA-approved drugs have been controversial, and there are studies that seem to support the value of natural medicines.

One dangerous assumption is the belief that something labeled "natural" cannot harm you. In fact, many natural

Natural remedies are not regulated by the FDA.

antidepressants react dangerously with prescription medications, so persons taking natural antidepressants should always tell their doctor before receiving any prescription. Many of today's doctors are familiar with nonprescription treatments and how they will react with prescription drugs.

St. John's wort is a "natural" antidepressant.

There are a number of commonly available natural reme-dies for depression. These include kava, 5-HTP, ginkgo biloba, and a variety of vitamins. One of the most highly acclaimed is St. John's wort.

St. John's Wort

One of today's most popular remedies for depression is in fact an ancient medicine. St. John's wort (botanical name *Hypericum perforatum*) was used as a cure by ancient Greeks and medieval monks. Numerous sufferers from depression credit this small woodland plant with relieving their unhappiness, and it has been widely studied, especially in Europe. In 1994, St. John's wort outsold Prozac by a twenty-to-one ratio in Germany.

Though you might think that with thousands of years of use and great popularity, *Hypericum* would be proven effec-tive as treatment for depression, the jury is still out on the effectiveness of the little plant. Some studies have shown the wort to be as effective as antidepressants, while others sug-gest it is no more effective than a placebo. Doctors Laurel L. Smith and Charles H. Elliot conclude, "The conclusion you can make from these studies as a whole is that St. John's wort is probably an effective treatment for mild depression for some people."

Meditation, Spiritual Practices, and Depression

Some time-honored practices from the East may be help-ful for treating depression. Professor Mark Williams of the

Department of Psychology at the University of Wales studied the effects of meditation on depression. Williams's findings show that people who have had repeated bouts of depression in the year following an eight-week course of meditation are twice as likely not to suffer a recurrence as those with no treatment. There is also anecdotal evidence that the breathing and stretching exercises of yoga may relieve depression—a treatment suggested five thousand years ago in the Vedas.

Some studies suggest a positive connection between spiritual beliefs and treatment of depression. For most of the twentieth century, therapists considered religiosity as more cause than cure for depression. More recently, psychiatrist Richard Flach, author of *The Secret Strength of Depression*, cites studies that "indicate that people who are more religiously active have fewer depressive symptoms" than those without strong spiritual beliefs. Dr. Flach emphasizes that religiosity is by no means insurance against depression as "the experience of depression . . . is practically universal." Yet "religious coping . . . appears to **mitigate** . . . symptoms of depression." So, for those who hold some form of spiritual belief, continuing to practice customary spiritual rituals may help combat the illness.

Exercise and Diet

Regular exercise that elevates your heart and respiration rates has been shown to be an effective treatment of both depression and anxiety. "Runner's high" is a reality—but you don't have to run marathons to experience the emotional benefits

*Meditation and other spiritual practices
may help combat depression.*

of exercise. A diet that includes a healthy balance of all the food groups and that is high in fiber can also contribute to better mental health.

A New High-Tech Treatment

Transcranial magnetic stimulation (TMS) is a new experimental treatment for depression. An electric coil is placed on a patient's head. The coil produces a magnetic field, which is targeted to specific portions of the brain. This treatment is still in its infancy, but early studies suggest TMS may produce the beneficial effects of ECT without the memory loss that sometimes accompanies electroshock.

Depression Is Still a Mystery and a Challenge

This history of depression and its treatment leads to several observations. First, depression is a complex and challenging affliction, involving both mental and biological components; it is darkness both of body and mind. After more than two thousand years of study, few scientists claim to fully understand the illness. Furthermore, the best efforts of psychologists and psychiatrists have failed to produce any single treatment that is 100 percent effective. Because there are several forms of the illness and innumerable differences between individual patients, treatments must be very carefully matched to each person. This by no means suggests that research has been in vain; today's treatments for depression are vastly superior to the crude and superstitious treatments of the past.

At the beginning of 2006, studies continue to indicate that depression is best treated with a dual approach: a combination of psychotherapy and antidepressant medication offering the best hope of relief.

Further Reading

Ainsworth, Patricia. *Understanding Depression: A Solid Resource for Those Who Know Depression Personally and for Those Who Want to Understand Them.* Jackson: University Press of Mississippi, 2000.

Cobain, Bev. *When Nothing Matters Anymore: A Survival Guide for Depressed Teens.* Minneapolis, Minn.: Free Spirit, 2004.

Dudley, William, ed. *The History of Drugs: Antidepressants.* Farmington Hills, Mich.: Greenhaven, 2005.

Elliot, Charles H., and Laura L. Smith. *Depression for Dummies.* Indianapolis: Wiley, 2003.

Fink, Max. *Healing Mental Illness: Electroshock.* New York: Oxford, 2003.

Greenfield, Susan A. *The Human Brain: A Guided Tour.* New York: Basic Books, 2005.

Knishinsky, Ran. *The Prozac Alternative: Natural Relief from Depression with St. John's Wort, Kava, Ginkgo, 5-HTP, Homeopathy, and Other Alternative Remedies.* Rochester, Vt.: Healing Arts Press, 1998.

For More Information

American Scientist Online: electroshock revisited by Max Fink
http://www.americanscientist.org/template/AssetDetail/assctid/26501

Depression & Mental Health: A Harvard Report
http://www.bhg.com/bhg/category.jhtml?categoryid = /templatedata/lhj/category/data/Health_Depression.xml

Electroboy: electroshock therapy
http://www.electroboy.com/electroshock-therapy.shtml

Focus Adolescent Services: Teen Suicide
http://www.focusas.com/Suicide.html

Gale Encyclopedia of Childhood and Adolescence: Depression
http://www.findarticles.com/p/articles/mi_g2602/is_0001/ai_2602000186

Medline Plus: Adolescent Depression
http://www.nlm.nih.gov/medlineplus/ency/article/001518.htm

National Mental Health Association: Adolescent Depression
http://www.nmha.org/infoctr/factsheets/24.cfm

Psychiatry online: How did pre-twentieth century theories
of the aetiology of depression develop? by Mead Mathews
http://www.priory.com/homol/dephist.htm

University of Illinois Counseling Center: Understanding
Depression
http://www.couns.uiuc.edu/Brochures/depress.htm

Publisher's note:
The Web sites listed on these pages were active at the time of publication.
The publisher is not responsible for Web sites that have changed their
addresses or discontinued operation since the date of publication. The
publisher will review and update the Web-site list upon each reprint.

Glossary

bile: According to medieval medicine, one of the four basic fluids of the body.

clinical depression: Depression that can be observed in a clinical setting.

dysthymic: Characteristic of a mild, chronic depression.

efficacy: Ability to produce necessary or desired results.

endogenous: Originating within an organism.

executor: Someone who carries out the instructions contained within a will.

grandiosity: An absurd and exaggerated sense of one's own splendor and importance.

hormones: Chemicals produced in a body's glands or cells that regulate or stimulate an effect.

humors: In medieval medicine, the four basic fluids in a body.

intravenous: Administered through a vein.

lithium: A chemical element that is used in compounds as a medical treatment for depression.

melancholia: An archaic term for depression.

Mesopotamia: An ancient region located between the Tigris and Euphrates rivers in what is now Iraq and Syria.

mitigate: To make something less harsh.

neurobiological: Relating to the nervous system and nerve cells.

pineal gland: A small, cone-shaped organ in the brain that secretes melatonin.

postpartum: Occurring after birth.

psychopharmacology: The scientific study of the effects of drugs on thought and behavior.

psychosis: A psychiatric disorder characterized by delusions, hallucinations, incoherence, and distorted perceptions of reality.

psychosocial: Relating to the psychological and social aspects of something.

rationality: The condition in which values, beliefs, and techniques are based on logical, explicable principles.

sexism: Discrimination based on gender.

St. John's wort: A small plant that has been used for medicinal purposes, including the treatment of depression.

stigma: Shame or disgrace attached to something regarded as socially unacceptable.

veritable: Indicating that something being referred to figuratively is as good as true.

Bibliography

ABC Health. Meditation and Depression. http://www. abc.net.au/dimensions/dimensions_health/Transcripts/ s533479.htm.

American Academy of Family Physicians. Cognitive Therapy for Depression. http://www.aafp.org/afp/20060101/83.html.

Famous People Who Have Suffered from Depression or Manic-depression. http://www.geocities.com/coverbridge2k/ artsci/famous_people_depression.html.

FDA Talk Paper. Antidepressant Use by Adults. http:// www.fda.gov/bbs/topics/ANSWERS/2005/ANS01362.html.

Flach, Frederic. *The Secret Strength of Depression*. New York: Hatherleigh Press, 2002.

History of Medicine in India: The Evolution of Psychology and Psychiatry. http://www.histmedindia.org/psy.htm.

Jackson, Stanley W. *Melancholia & Depression from Hippocratic Times to Modern Times*. New Haven, Conn.: Yale University Press, 1986.

Janick, Jules. *The History of Horticulture.* Purdue University. http://www.hort.purdue.edu/newcrop/history/lecture23/ lec23l.html.

Kansas State Historical Society: Patent Medicines. http:// www.kshs.org/portraits/patent_medicines.htm.

Medicine in Ancient Egypt. http://www.arabworldbooks. com/articles8c.htm.

Morbidly Hollywood. The Murder of Phil Hartman. http:// www.franksreelreviews.com/shorttakes/hartman.htm.

PBS. *Bloodletting Over the Centuries.* http://www.pbs.org/ wnet/redgold/basics/bloodlettinghistory.html.

Senior Care Services. Depression Among the Elderly. http:// seniorcareservices.org/depression_among_the_elderly.htm.

Web MD. Brooke Shield's Struggle with Postpartum Depression. http://www.webmd.com/content/article/104/107292. htm.

Index

Picture Credits

Benjamin Stewart: pp. 60, 71, 99
iStockphotos: pp. 72, 74, 87
　　Alejandro Raymond: p. 90
　　Andrei Tchernov: p. 64
　　Andrew Krasnov: p. 81
　　Brandon Gillette: p. 26
　　Dave Rau: p. 8
　　David Dycus: p. 66
　　Dena Steiner: p. 82
　　Diane Diederich: p. 62
　　Elena Ray: p. 32
　　Govinda Trazo: p. 100
　　Jacob Jensen: p. 96
　　Joshua Blake: p. 17
　　Julie Felton: p. 84
　　Konstaninos Kokkinis: p. 24
　　Lynn Watson: p. 104
　　Mads Abildgaard: p. 68
　　Martynas Juchnevicius: p. 78
　　Miroslaw Pieprzyk: p. 56
　　Sharon Dominick: p. 18
　　Sonja Foos: p. 55
Jupiter Images: pp. 13, 23, 92, 103, 107

Biographies

Author

Kenneth McIntosh is a freelance writer and teacher living in Northern Arizona. He has written two dozen educational books, and taught at junior high, high school, and community college levels.

Consultant

Andrew M. Kleiman, M.D., received a Bachelor of Arts degree in philosophy from the University of Michigan, and earned his medical degree from Tulane University School of Medicine. Dr. Kleiman completed his internship, residency in psychiatry, and fellowship in forensic psychiatry at New York University and Bellevue Hospital. He is currently in private practice in Manhattan, specializing in psychopharmacology, psychotherapy, and forensic psychiatry. He also teaches clinical psychology at the New York University School of Medicine.